CHARTED CHRISTMAS DESIGNS
for Counted Cross-Stitch and Other Needlecrafts

From
the Archives of the
Lindberg Press

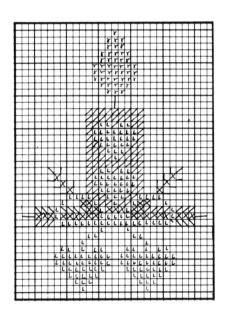

DOVER PUBLICATIONS, INC.
NEW YORK

Copyright © 1982 by Dover Publications, Inc.
All rights reserved under Pan American and International Copyright Conventions.

Published in Canada by General Publishing Company, Ltd., 30 Lesmill Road, Don Mills, Toronto, Ontario.
Published in the United Kingdom by Constable and Company, Ltd., 10 Orange Street, London WC2H 7EG.

Charted Christmas Designs for Counted Cross-Stitch and Other Needlecrafts, first published by Dover Publications, Inc., in 1982, is a new collection of charted designs from the archives of the Lindberg Press, Copenhagen, Denmark.

Manufactured in the United States of America
Dover Publications, Inc.,
180 Varick Street, New York, N.Y. 10014

Library of Congress Cataloging in Publication Data
Main entry under title:

Charted Christmas designs for counted cross-stitch and other needlecrafts.

(Dover needlework series)
1. Needlework—Patterns. 2. Cross-stitch—Patterns. 3. Christmas decorations. I. Lindberg Press. II. Series.
TT753.C46 1982   746.4   82-7308
ISBN 0-486-24356-7 (pbk.)   AACR2

Introduction

The Christmas holiday season is a time of sharing and giving. Probably the most meaningful gifts and beautiful decorations are those made with the care and attention that only a handmade item can receive. This book of charted designs is filled with ideas that will add a distinctive, personal touch to your Christmas gift-giving and decorating.

All of the designs are charted for ready use in different forms of needlework such as counted cross-stitch, needlepoint, latch-hooking, crochet and knitting. To give inspiration, many of the designs are shown on the covers as completed projects. You can make the items shown or use the charts to create your own needlework designs. Combine several small motifs to make an unusual Christmas sampler or tree skirt. Use a border design to embroider matching cuffs, collar and yoke for a new Christmas dress. Embellish the pocket of your favorite holiday apron with some mischievous pixies. Latch-hook some of the more elaborate designs to create an inviting hearth rug or pillow. Knit a snowflake design into your next stockinette-stitch sweater, or crochet an afghan and embellish it with poinsettias and holly. As you can see, the possibilities are as wonderful as they are endless!

Keep in mind that the finished piece of needlework will not be the same size as the charted design unless you happen to be working on fabric (or canvas) that has the same number of threads per inch as the chart has squares per inch. With knitting and crocheting, the size will vary according to the number of stitches per inch.

To determine how large a finished counted cross-stitch design will be, divide the number of stitches in the design by the thread-count of the fabric. For example, if a design that is 112 stitches wide by 140 stitches deep is worked on a 14-count cloth, divide 112 stitches by 14 to get 8 and 140 by 14 to get 10; so the worked design will measure 8″ x 10″. The same design worked on 22-count fabric would measure approximately 5″ x 6½″.

Most of these designs were originally created for counted cross-stitch; one of the great advantages to this craft is that the supplies and equipment required are minimal and inexpensive. You will need:

1. A small blunt tapestry needle, # 24 or # 26.

2. Evenweave fabric. This can be linen, cotton, wool or a blend that includes miracle fibers. The three most popular fabrics are:

Cotton Aida. This is made 14 threads per inch, 11 threads per inch, 8 threads per inch, and so forth. Fourteen, being the prettiest, is preferred.

Evenweave Linen. This also comes in a variety of threads per inch. Working on evenweave linen involves a slightly different technique, which is explained on page 5. Thirty-count linen will give a stitch approximately the same size as 14-count aida.

Hardanger Cloth. This has 22 threads per inch and is available in cotton or linen.

3. Embroidery thread. This can be six-strand mercerized cotton floss (DMC, Coats and Clark, Lily, Anchor, etc.), crewel wool, Danish Flower Thread, silken and metal threads or pearl cotton. DMC embroidery thread has been used to color-code all of the patterns in this book. One skein of each color given in the color key is needed, unless otherwise indicated in parentheses). For 14-count aida and 30-count linen, divide six-strand cotton floss and work with only two strands. For more texture, use more thread; for a flatter look, use less thread. Crewel wool is pretty on an evenweave wool fabric, and some embroiderers even use wool on cotton fabric. Danish Flower Thread is a thicker thread with a matte finish, one strand equaling two of cotton floss.

4. Embroidery hoop. Use a plastic or wooden 4″, 5″ or 6″ round or oval hoop with a screw type tension adjuster.

5. A pair of sharp embroidery scissors is absolutely essential.

Prepare the fabric by whipping, hemming or zigzagging on the sewing machine to prevent raveling at the edges. Next, locate the exact center of the design you have chosen, so that you can then center the design on the piece of fabric. Many of the designs in the book have an arrow at the top and along one side; follow the indicated rows to where they intersect; this is the center stitch. Next, find the center of the fabric by folding it in half both vertically and horizontally. The center stitch of the design should fall where the creases in the fabric meet.

It's usually not very convenient to begin work with the center stitch itself. As a rule it's better to start at the top of a design, working horizontal rows of a single color, left to right. This technique permits you to go from an unoccupied space to an occupied space (from an empty hole to a filled one), which makes ruffling the floss less likely. To find out where the top of the design should be placed, count squares up from the center of the design, and then count off the corresponding number of holes up from the center of the fabric.

Next, place the section of the fabric to be worked tautly in the hoop; the tighter the better, for tension makes it easier to push the needle through the holes without piercing the fabric. As you work, use the screw adjuster to tighten as necessary. Keep the screw at the top and out of your way.

Counted cross-stitch is very simple. When beginning, fasten thread with a waste knot by holding a bit of thread on the underside of the work and anchoring it with the first few stitches (*diagram 1*). To stitch, push the threaded needle up

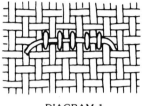

DIAGRAM 1
Reverse side of work

through a hole in the fabric and cross over the thread intersection (or square) diagonally, left to right (*diagram 2*). This

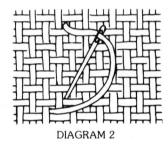

DIAGRAM 2

is half the stitch. Now cross back, right to left, making an X (*diagram 3*). Do all the stitches in the same color in the same

DIAGRAM 3

row, working left to right and slanting from bottom left to upper right (*diagram 3*). Then cross back, completing the X's (*diagram 4*). Some cross-stitchers prefer to cross each stitch

DIAGRAM 4

as they come to it; this is fine, but be sure the slant is always in the correct direction. Of course, isolated stitches must be crossed as you work them. Vertical stitches are crossed as shown in diagram 5. Holes are used more than once; all

DIAGRAM 5

stitches "hold hands" unless a space is indicated. The work is always held upright, never turned as for some needlepoint stitches.

When carrying a color from one area to another, wiggle your needle under existing stitches on the underside. Do not carry a color across an open expanse of fabric for more than a few stitches, as the thread will be visible from the front. Remember, in counted cross-stitch you do not work the background.

To end a color, weave in and out of the underside of stitches, perhaps making a scallop stitch or two for extra security (*diagram 6*). Whenever possible, end in the direction

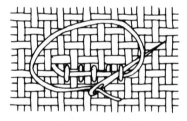

DIAGRAM 6
Reverse side of work

in which you are traveling, jumping up a row if necessary (*diagram 7*). This prevents holes caused by work being pulled in two directions. Do not make knots; knots make

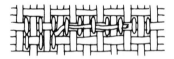

DIAGRAM 7
Reverse side of work

bumps. Cut off the ends of the threads; do not leave any tails because they'll show through when the work is mounted.

Another stitch used in counted cross-stitch is the back-

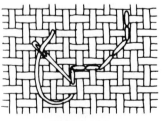

DIAGRAM 8

stitch. This is worked from hole to hole and may be vertical, horizontal or slanted (*diagram 8*). For a special effect, chain stitch or lazy daisy stitch may be recommended; these stitches can be worked in the normal fashion (*diagram 9*).

LAZY DAISY   CHAIN STITCH

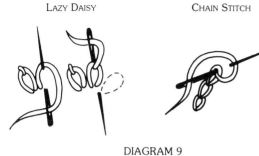

DIAGRAM 9

Working on linen requires a slightly different technique. Evenweave linen is remarkably regular, but there are always some thin threads and some that are nubbier or fatter than others. To even these out and to make a stitch that is easy to see, the cross-stitch is worked over two threads each way. The "square" you are covering is thus 4 threads (*diagram 10*). The first few stitches on linen are sometimes difficult, but one quickly begins "to see in twos." After the third stitch, a

DIAGRAM 10

pattern is established, and should you inadvertently cross over three threads instead of four, the difference in slant will make it immediately apparent that you have erred.

Linen evenweave fabric should be worked with the selvage at the side, not at the top and bottom.

Because you go over more threads, linen affords more variations in stitches. A half stitch can slant in either direction and is uncrossed. A three-fourths stitch is shown in diagram 11. Diagram 12 shows backstitch on linen.

Gingham or other checkered material can also be used for counted cross-stitch by making the crosses over the checks from corner to corner. If you wish to embroider a cross-stitch design onto a fabric that does not have an even weave, baste

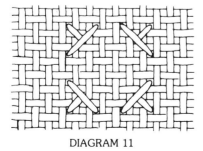

DIAGRAM 11

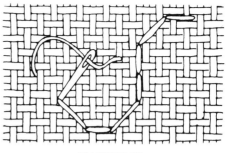

DIAGRAM 12

a lightweight Penelope canvas to the fabric. The design can then be worked from the chart by making crosses over the double mesh of the canvas, being careful not to catch the threads of the canvas in the sewing. When the design is completed, the basting stitches are removed, and the horizontal and then the vertical threads of the canvas are removed, one strand at a time, with a tweezers. The cross-stitch design will remain on the fabric.

After you have completed your embroidery, wash it in cool or lukewarm water with a mild soap. Rinse well. Do not wring. Roll in a towel to remove excess moisture. Immediately iron on a padded surface with the embroidery face down. Be sure the embroidery is completely dry before attempting to mount it.

To mount as a picture, center the embroidery over a pure white, rag-content mat board. Turn margins over to the back evenly. Lace the margins with sturdy thread, top to bottom, side to side. The fabric should be tight and even, with a little tension. Never use glue for mounting. Counted cross-stitch on cotton or linen may be framed under glass. Wool needs to breathe and should not be framed under glass unless a breathing space is left.

Charted designs can also be used for needlepoint. The designs can be worked directly onto needlepoint canvas by counting off the correct number of warp and weft squares shown on the chart, each square representing one stitch to be taken on the canvas. If you prefer to put some guidelines on the canvas, make certain that your marking medium is waterproof. Use either nonsoluble inks, acrylic paints thinned appropriately with water so as not to clog the holes in the canvas, or oil paints mixed with benzine or turpentine. Felt-tipped pens are very handy, but check the labels carefully because not all felt markers are waterproof. It is a good idea to experiment with any writing materials on a piece of scrap canvas to make certain that all material is waterproof. There is nothing worse than having a bit of ink run onto the needlepoint as you are blocking it.

There are two distinct types of needlepoint canvas: single-mesh and double-mesh. Double-mesh is woven with two horizontal and two vertical threads forming each mesh, whereas single-mesh is woven with one vertical and one horizontal thread forming each mesh. Double-mesh is a very stable canvas on which the threads will stay securely in place as you work. Single-mesh canvas, which is more widely used, is a little easier on the eyes because the spaces are slightly larger.

A tapestry needle with a rounded, blunt tip and an elongated eye is used for needlepoint. The most commonly used needle for #10 canvas is the #18 needle. The needle should clear the hole in the canvas without spreading the threads. Special yarns that have good twist and are sufficiently heavy to cover the canvas are used for needlepoint.

Although there are over a hundred different needlepoint

stitches, the *Tent Stitch* is universally considered to be *the* needlepoint stitch. The three most familiar versions of Tent Stitch are: Plain Half-Cross Stitch, Continental Stitch and Basket Weave Stitch.

Plain Half-Cross Stitch *(diagram 13)*. Always work Half-Cross Stitch from left to right, then turn the canvas around and work the return row, still stitching from left to right. Bring the needle to the front of the canvas at a point that will be the bottom of the first stitch. The needle is in a vertical position when making the stitch. Keep the stitches loose for minimum distortion and good coverage. This stitch must be worked on a double-mesh canvas.

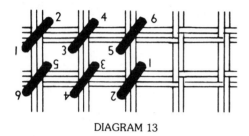

DIAGRAM 13

Continental Stitch *(diagram 14)*. Start this design at the upper right-hand corner and work from right to left. The needle is slanted and always brought out a mesh ahead. The resulting stitch is actually a Half-Cross Stitch on top and a slanting stitch on the back. When the row is finished, turn the canvas around and work the return row, still stitching from right to left.

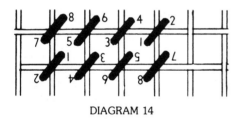

DIAGRAM 14

Basket Weave Stitch *(diagram 15)*. Start in the upper right-hand corner of the area with four Continental Stitches, two worked horizontally across the top and two placed directly below the first stitch. Then work diagonal rows, the first slanting up and across the canvas from right to left and the next down and across from left to right. Each new row is

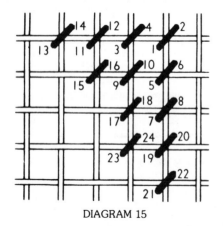

DIAGRAM 15

one stitch longer. As you go down the canvas (left to right), the needle is held in a vertical position; as you move in the opposite direction, the needle is horizontal. The rows should interlock, creating a basket-weave pattern on the reverse. If this is not done properly, a faint ridge will show where the pattern was interrupted. Always stop working in the middle of a row, rather than at the end, so that you will know in which direction you are working.

Bind all the raw edges of needlepoint canvas with masking tape, double-fold bias tape or even adhesive tape. There are no set rules on where to begin a design. Generally it is easier to begin close to the center and work outward toward the edges of the canvas, working the backgrounds or borders last. To avoid fraying the yarn, work with strands not longer than 18″.

When you have finished your needlepoint, it should be blocked. No matter how straight you have kept your work, blocking will give it a professional look.

Any hard, flat surface that you do not mind marring with nail holes and one that will not be warped by wet needlepoint can serve as a blocking board. A large piece of plywood, an old drawing board or an old-fashioned doily blocker are ideal.

Moisten a Turkish towel in cold water and roll the needlepoint in the towel. Leaving the needlepoint in the towel overnight will insure that both the canvas and the yarn are thoroughly and evenly dampened. Do not saturate the needlepoint! Never hold the needlepoint under the faucet as that much water is not necessary.

Mark the desired outline on the blocking board, making sure that the corners are straight. Lay the needlepoint on the blocking board, and tack the canvas with thumbtacks spaced about ½″ to ¾″ apart. It will probably take a good deal of pulling and tugging to get the needlepoint straight, but do not be afraid of this stress. Leave the canvas on the blocking board until thoroughly dry. Never put an iron on your needlepoint. You cannot successfully block with a steam iron because the needlepoint must dry in the straightened position. You may also have needlepoint blocked professionally. If you have a pillow made, a picture framed or a chair seat mounted, the craftsman may include the blocking in the price.

Charted designs can be worked in duplicate stitch over the squares formed by stockinette stitch in knitting or afghan stitch in crochet. The patterns can also be knitted directly into the work by working with more than one color, as in Fair Isle knitting. The wool not in use is always stranded across the back of the work. When it has to be stranded over more than five stitches, it should be twisted around the wool in use on every third stitch, thus preventing long strands at the back of the work. When several colors are used, a method known as "motif knitting" is employed. In this method short lengths of wool are cut and wound on bobbins, using a separate bobbin for each color and twisting the colors where they meet to avoid gaps in the work, as in knitting argyle socks.

Each of the designs has its own color key. The colors, however, are merely suggestions. You should feel free to substitute your own colors for the ones indicated, thereby creating a design that is uniquely yours. If you decide to create a new color scheme, work it out in detail before beginning a project. To give you a good idea of how the finished project will look, put tracing paper over the design in the book and experiment with your own colors on the tracing paper.

CHRISTMAS SAMPLER

Shown in color on the front cover.

DMC #

⊙	704	pale kelly green	◨◪ 782	light coffee	⊡ 761	light rose
②	702	medium kelly green	▽ 809	medium Dresden blue	◨ 352	medium peach
▼	741	medium yellow-orange	◪ 798	dark Dresden blue	◗◖ 350	dark peach
◨◪	743	dark lemon yellow *(backstitch: angel's halo and treetop)*	■ 797	royal blue	☒ 666	scarlet

7

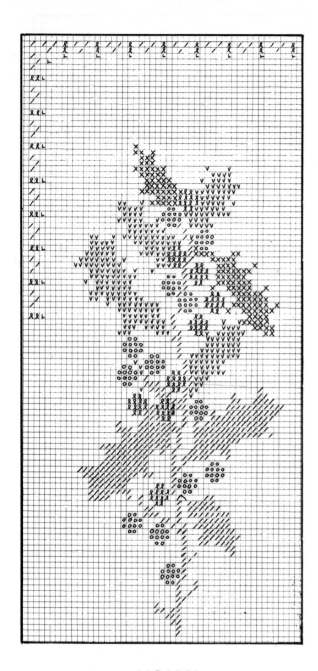

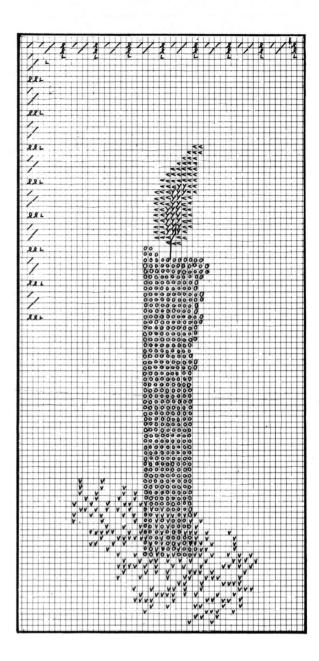

HOLLY

Shown in color on the inside back cover.

	DMC #	
⊠	913	light malachite green
Ⓥ	911	medium malachite green
⊠	910	deep malachite green
⊙	321	light ruby
⊠	666	scarlet
Ⓛ	742	light yellow-orange

RED CANDLE

Shown in color on the inside back cover.

	DMC #	
Ⓥ	911	medium malachite green
⊠	910	deep malachite green
⊙	321	light ruby
⊠	666	scarlet
⊠	743	dark lemon yellow
Ⓛ	742	light yellow-orange
⊠	741	medium yellow-orange
	310	black (*backstitch: wick*)

ORNAMENTS

Shown in color on the inside back cover.

DMC #

☒	913	light malachite green
☑	911	medium malachite green (*backstitch: hangers*)
◪	910	deep malachite green
◉	321	light ruby
☒	666	scarlet
⊡	307	medium yellow
◿	743	dark lemon yellow
⌊	742	light yellow-orange
☒	741	medium yellow-orange
◢	797	royal blue

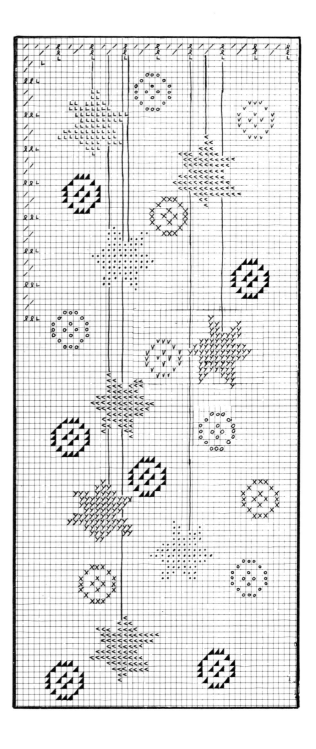

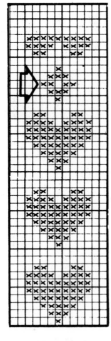

BORDER
DESIGN

See pages 11-13 for charts.

HAPPY HOLIDAY
SCENES

Shown in color on the inside front cover.

	DMC #	
⊡		snow white
⊟	422	beige
⊠	435	bright tan
③	434	dark tan
⊂	973	canary yellow
⊔	740	dark yellow-orange
⊅	972	light orange
⊡	353	light peach
⊟	760	medium rose
▼	718	light red-violet (2)
◪	498	dark ruby
⌀	603	dark hot pink
⊠	666	scarlet (9) *(backstitch: mouths)*
Ⅱ	798	dark Dresden blue (2)
⊠	995	bright electric blue *(backstitch: ╫ and heavy outlines on girl's dress and sleeve in second heart)*
⊻	732	medium olive green *(backstitch: heavy outlines on girl's clothes in first heart)*
⊠	906	medium emerald green (2)
⊠	3345	hunter green
◖	895	dark hunter green (5) *(backstitch: ·····)*
⊤	318	light gray
⊠	317	dark gray *(backstitch: ━)*
◉	310	black *(backstitch: ∿∿ and outline of dog in second heart)*

first heart

second heart

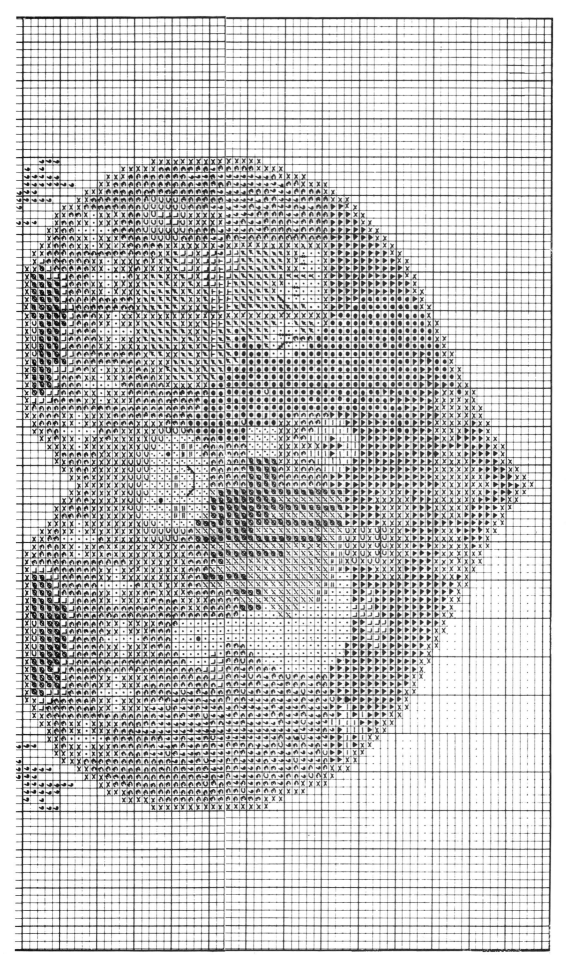

third heart

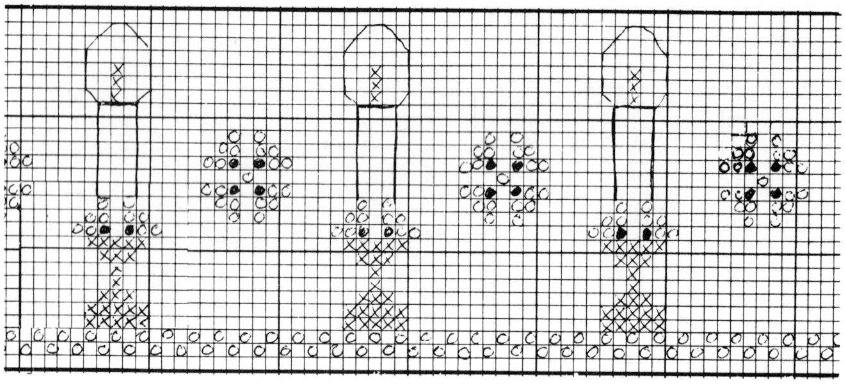

CANDLE BORDER

Shown in color on the back cover.

	DMC #	
☐		snow white
◙	703	light kelly green
◼	700	dark kelly green
☒	973	canary yellow (*backstitch: halo*)

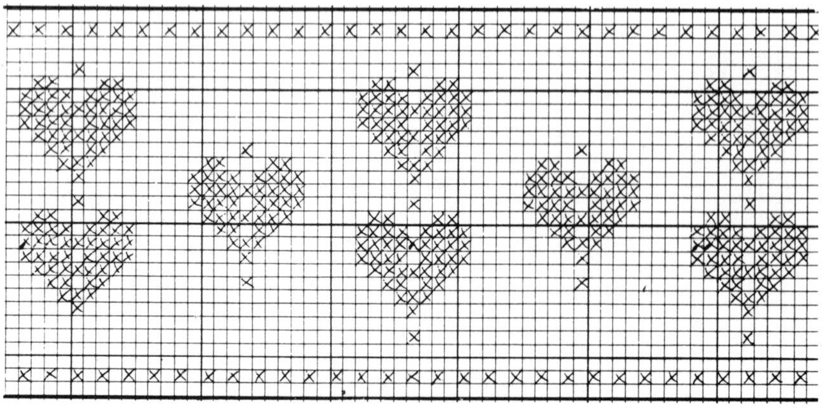

HEART BORDER

	DMC #	
☒	666	scarlet

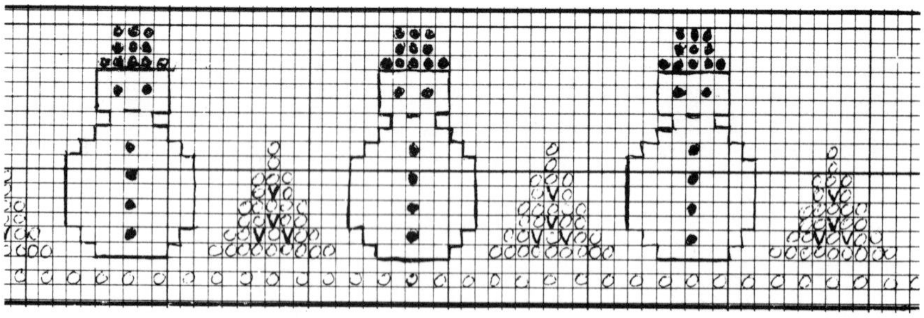

SNOWMAN BORDER

Shown in color on the back cover.

	DMC #	
☐		snow white
V	666	scarlet
◙	701	bright kelly green
●	310	black (*backstitch: mouths*)

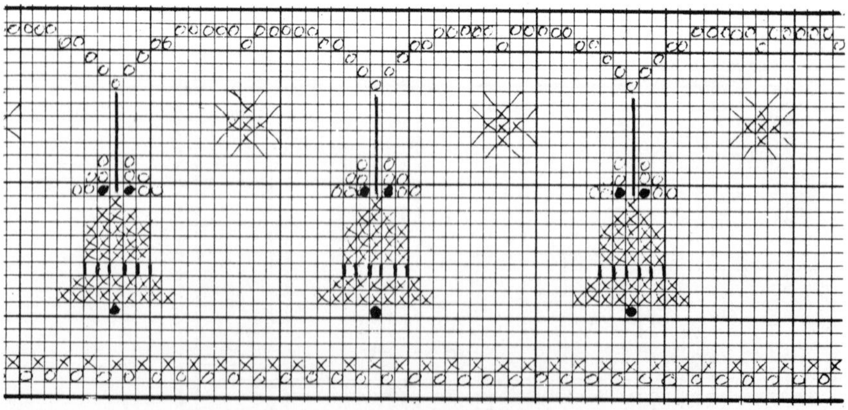

CHRISTMAS BELL BORDER

Shown in color on the inside back cover.

	DMC #	
☒		snow white (*backstitch: design on bell and halos around stars*)
●	310	black
◙	701	bright kelly green

PIXIE BORDER

Shown in color on the back cover.

DMC #

⊠ 666   scarlet (*backstitch: mouths*)

◉ 701   bright kelly green

⊙   snow white

   310   black (*backstitch: eyes*)

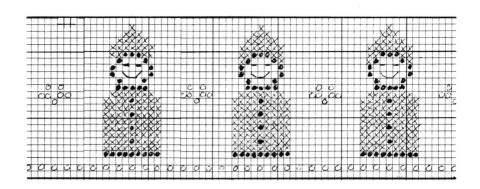

CHRISTMAS TREE BORDER

Shown in color on the inside back cover.

DMC #

⊠ 666   scarlet (*for hearts*)

⊠ 701   bright kelly green (*for trees*)

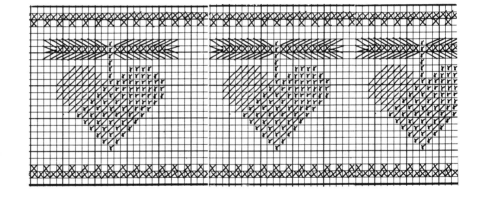

WOVEN HEART BORDER

DMC #

⊠ 701   bright kelly green (*backstitch: pine needles*)

⧄ 776   medium pink

⊠ 666   scarlet

CANDLE BORDER

Shown in color on the back cover.

DMC #

⊡ 973   canary yellow (*backstitch: halo and stars*)

⧄ 666   scarlet

⊠ 701   bright kelly green (*backstitch: pine needles*)

   310   black (*backstitch: wick*)

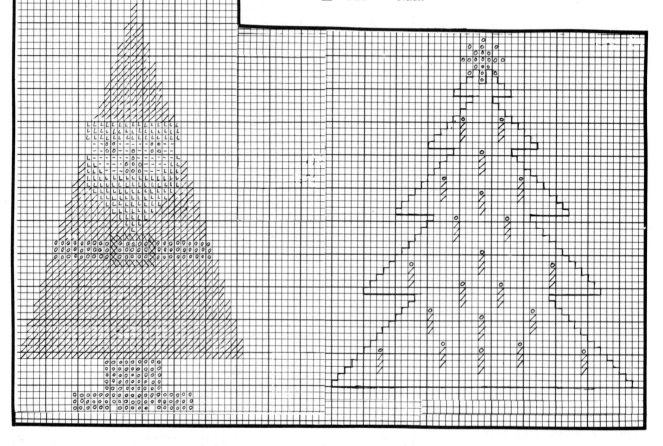

SANTA TABLE RUNNER

Shown in color on the inside back cover.

	DMC #	
Ⓛ		snow white
☒	973	canary yellow
◮	971	dark orange
◿	666	scarlet
⊟	422	beige
☐	702	medium kelly green
⊙	310	black

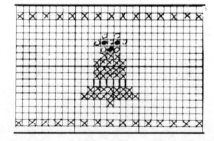

BELL MOTIF

	DMC #	
☒		snow white (backstitch: vertical stitches on bell)
⊙	666	scarlet
⊙	701	bright kelly green

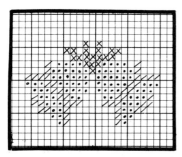

BELL NAPKIN RINGS

Shown in color on the front cover.

DMC #

⊡		snow white
⊿	762	pale gray
⊠	702	medium kelly green

CHRISTMAS BELL

DMC #

⊠		snow white
⊿	666	scarlet
U	701	bright kelly green
		(backstitch: hanger)

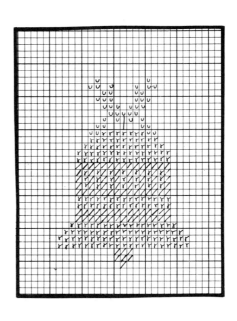

BELL WITH PINE BRANCHES

DMC #

⊠		snow white
⊙	415	silver gray
⊠	701	bright kelly green
		(backstitch: pine needles)

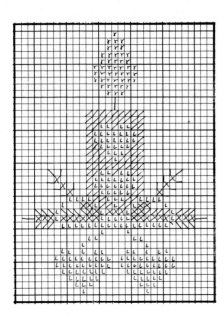

CANDLE
AND HEARTS

DMC #

⊠	973	canary yellow
⊿	776	medium pink
L	666	scarlet
⊠	699	deep kelly green

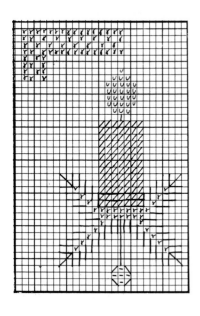

◀ CANDLE

DMC #

⊿		snow white
U	444	dark yellow
⊠	701	bright kelly green *(backstitch: pine needles)*
⊟	310	black *(backstitch: around hanging ornament and candle base)*

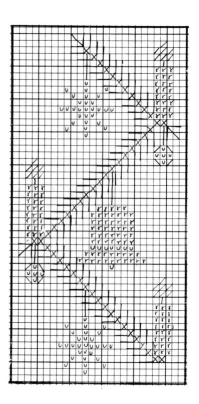

PINE, BELL AND
CANDLE HANGER

Shown in color on the inside front cover.

DMC #

⊿	742	light yellow-orange
⊠	700	dark kelly green
⊠		snow white
U	762	pale gray

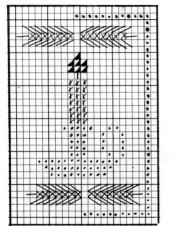

CANDLE WITH
PINE BRANCHES

DMC #

◣	742	light yellow-orange
⊠	604	medium hot pink
•	666	scarlet
⊠	702	medium kelly green *(backstitch: pine needles)*
Ⅱ	310	black

CANDLES AND SNOWFLAKES

DMC #

☒		snow white
L	762	pale gray
◪	972	light orange
☒	701	bright kelly green

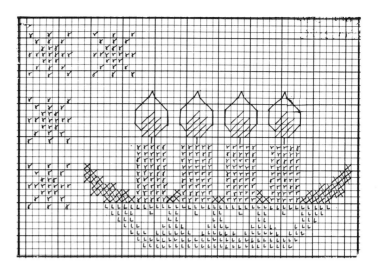

CANDLES, SNOWFLAKES AND HEARTS

DMC #

U	973	canary yellow
☒		snow white
◪	702	medium kelly green

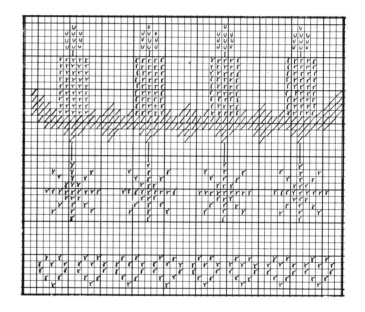

CANDLE WITH PINE

DMC #

·	743	dark lemon yellow
	742	light yellow-orange (backstitch: halo)
◪	741	medium yellow-orange
◎	666	scarlet
☒	911	medium malachite green
	310	black (backstitch: wick)

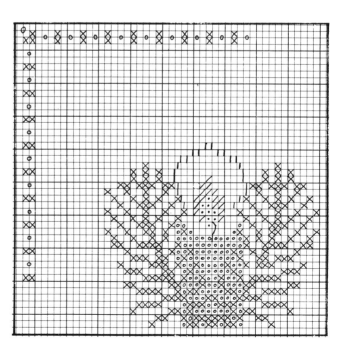

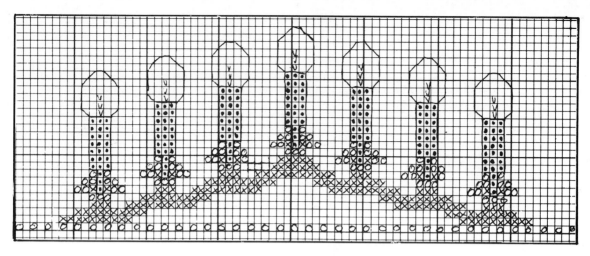

CANDELABRA

DMC #

⊡		snow white (backstitch: candle outlines)
☑	743	dark lemon yellow (backstitch: halo)
☒	666	scarlet
⊡	702	medium kelly green

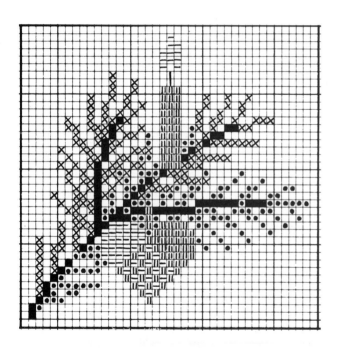

PINE, CANDLE AND HEART MOTIF

DMC #

⊟	972	light orange
⦿	608	orange-red
☒	906	medium emerald green
⊡	905	bright emerald green
■	831	light bronze
⧈	310	black

HEART AND PINE TABLE RUNNER ▶

Shown in color on the inside front cover.

DMC #

⊡	725	medium marigold (chain-stitch or lazy daisy-stitch: flames)
⊘	741	medium yellow-orange
⊐	900	dark pumpkin
⊙	606	dark orange-red
☒	989	light grass green
▼	841	dusty brown

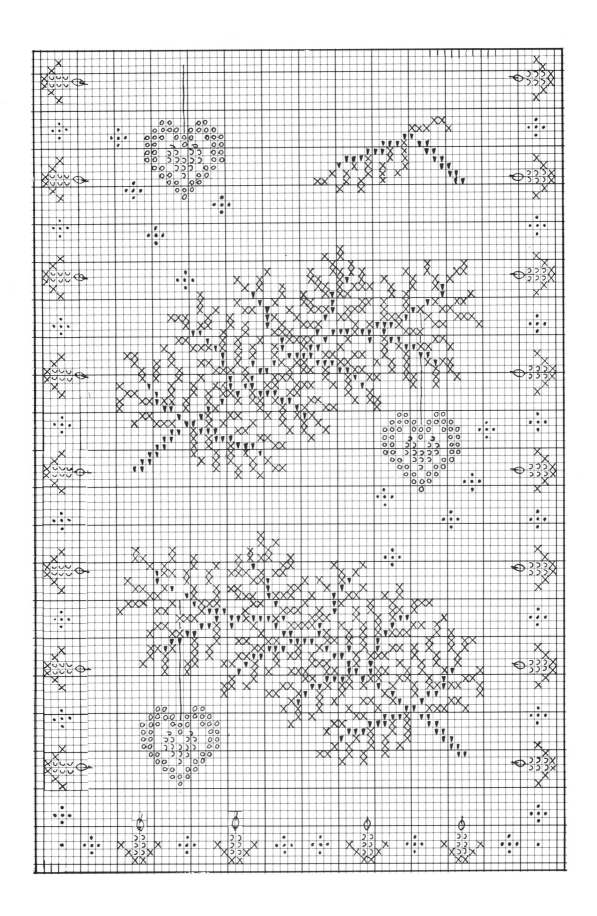

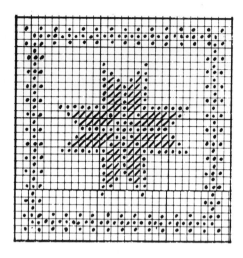

STAR MOTIF

DMC #
- ◩ 605   light hot pink
- ⊡ 666   scarlet

SNOWFLAKE

Shown in color on the front cover.

DMC #
- ⊠   snow white

STAR

DMC #
- ● 666   scarlet
- ⊠ 701   bright kelly green

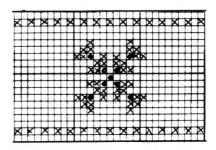

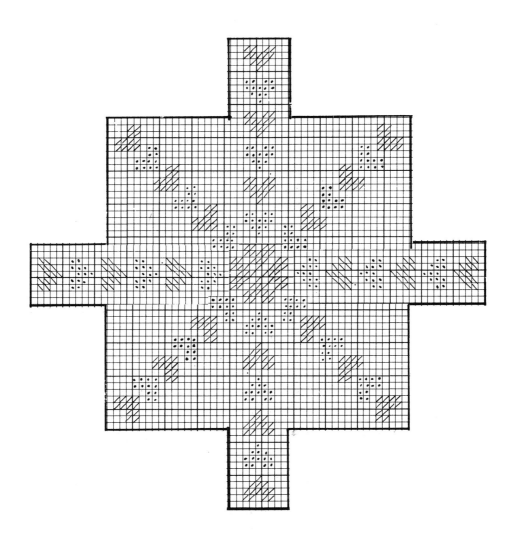

HEART SNOWFLAKE

DMC #
- ◪ ◩ 666   scarlet
- ⊡ 605   light hot pink

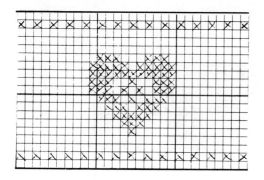

HEART

DMC #

⊠ 666   scarlet

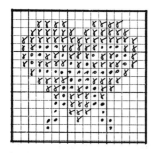

HEART MOTIF

DMC #

⊠ 433   light chocolate brown

▪ 666   scarlet

HEART CHRISTMAS TREE

Shown in color on the front cover.

DMC #

⊠ 666   scarlet (7)

⊠ 699   deep kelly green (5)
               *(backstitch: pine
               needles)*

⊘   metallic gold (1 spool)

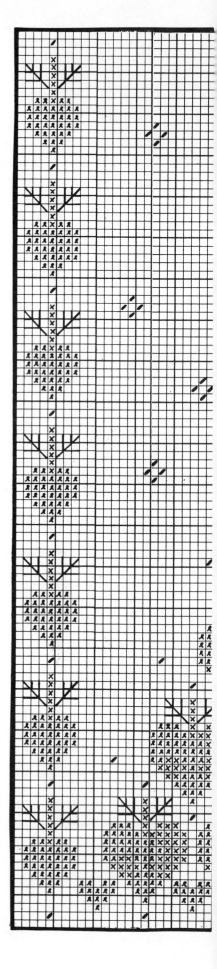

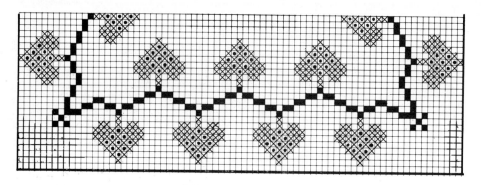

HEART BORDER

DMC #

⊡	947	light pumpkin
⊠	666	scarlet
■	701	bright kelly green

HEART WITH BORDER

DMC #

⊡	893	medium salmon
⊠	666	scarlet
⊠	995	bright electric blue
⊠	906	medium emerald green
◨ ⊠	904	dark emerald green

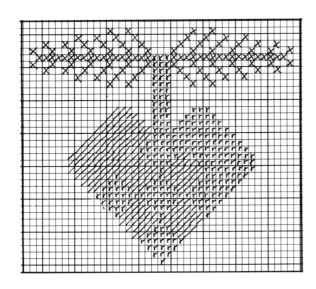

WOVEN HEART
WITH PINE

DMC #

⊿	605	light hot pink
⅄	321	light ruby
⊠	700	dark kelly green

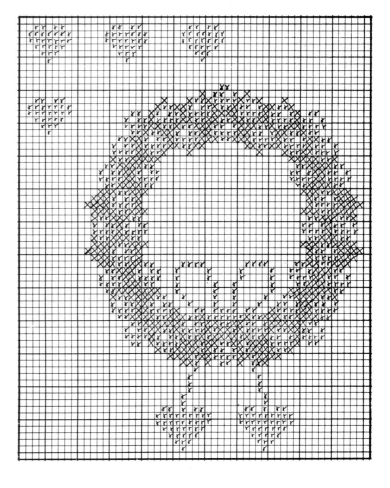

WREATH

DMC #

⊠	666	scarlet
⊠	702	medium kelly green

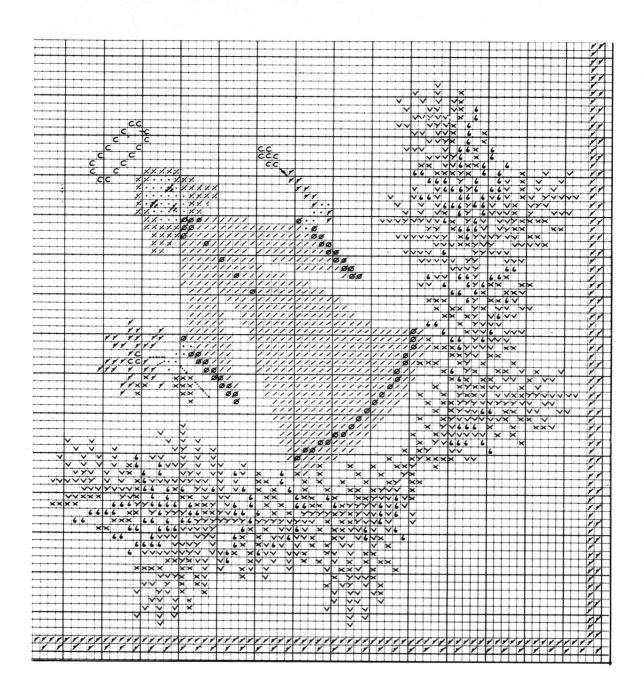

ANGEL
CORNER MOTIF

	DMC #				
·	754	medium flesh		825	deep blue
c	725	medium marigold	V	907	light emerald green
X	832	dark brass	X	906	medium emerald green (backstitch: •••••)
/	891	dark salmon (backstitch: mouth)	6	988	medium grass green
/	813	medium blue (backstitch: eyes)	X	781	medium coffee (backstitch: eyebrows)
Ø	826	bright blue		310	black (backstitch: wick)

ANGELS

Shown in color on the inside front cover.

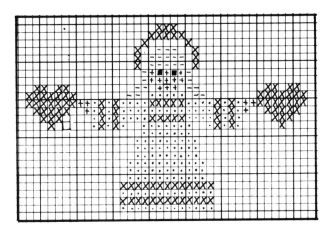

DMC #

·		snow white
⊠	725	medium marigold
⊞	948	flesh
■		black

ANGELS AND SNOWFLAKES

Shown in color on the inside front cover.

DMC #

⊞	754	medium flesh
⊟	307	medium yellow
⊿	554	light lilac OR
	3348	light spring green OR
	970	medium orange
⍟	718	light red-violet OR
	699	deep kelly green OR
	606	dark orange-red
⊠	725	medium marigold
⌊	666	scarlet (backstitch: mouth)
⋃	319	deep moss green
⊙	433	light chocolate brown (backstitch: wick)

To make hanging as shown in photograph, substitute candles and trees for hearts on second and third angels respectively; work angels in order of the listed colors for ⊿ and ⍟ .

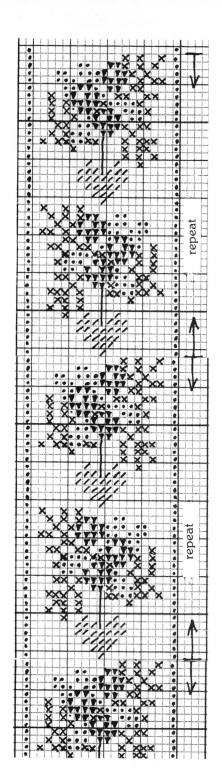

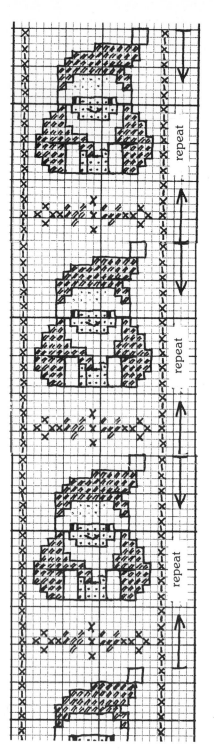

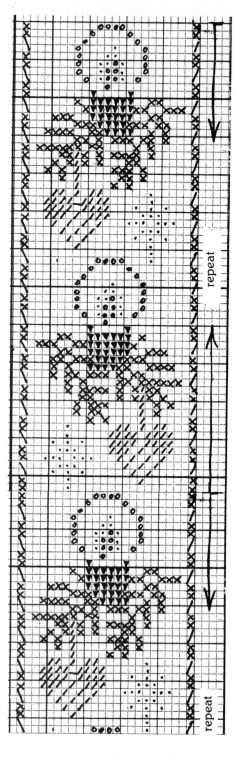

HOLLY AND HEARTS BORDER

Shown in color on the front cover.

DMC #

▼	666	scarlet
⧄	602	light magenta
⊡	906	medium emerald green
⊠	367	bright moss green

SANTA BORDER

Shown in color on the front cover.

DMC #

⧄	666	scarlet
⊡	224	light old rose
⊠	700	dark kelly green (back-stitch: border)
◧	310	black (backstitch: outline of Santa)

CANDLE BORDER

Shown in color on the front cover.

DMC #

⊡	973	canary yellow
⊙	970	medium orange
▼	666	scarlet (backstitch: border)
⧄	602	light magenta
⊠	700	dark kelly green

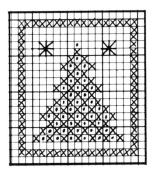

CHRISTMAS TREE MOTIF

DMC #

⊡ 725   medium marigold or metallic gold (back-stitch: stars)

☒ 702   medium kelly green

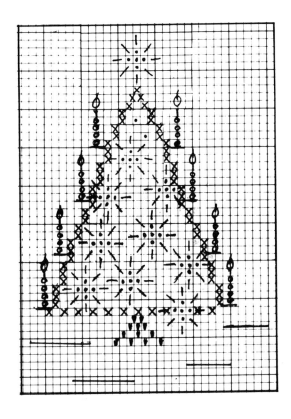

DECORATED CHRISTMAS TREE

DMC #

⊡ 973   canary yellow (back-stitch: halos)

♂ 970   medium orange (lazy daisy-stitch)

⊡ 666   scarlet (backstitch: candle base)

☒ 700   dark kelly green

▼ 433   light chocolate brown (backstitch: floor)

   310   black (backstitch: wick)

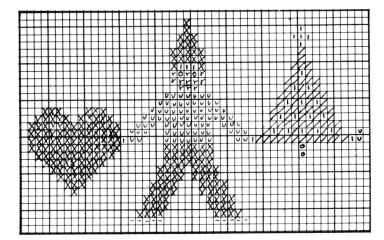

For a border design, continue working elves, trees and hearts (see hand on right side of tree for position of next elf).

ELF MOTIF

DMC #

☒ 739   ice brown

① 307   medium yellow

☒ 666   scarlet

Ⓤ 415   silver gray

☑ 701   bright kelly green

⊙ 433   bright chocolate brown

⊟ 310   black

JUMPING ELVES

Shown in color on the inside front cover.

DMC #

⊞ 754 medium flesh

Ⅱ 307 medium yellow

⧄ 666 scarlet

⊠ 699 deep kelly green

⧅ 318 light gray

⊟ 310 black

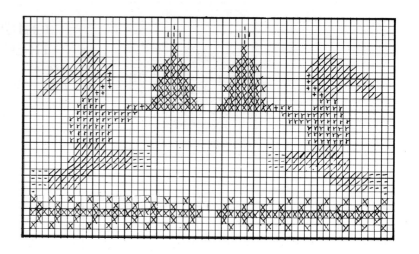

PIXIE TABLECLOTH AND MATCHBOXES

Shown in color on the inside front cover.

DMC #

⊡ 754 medium flesh

⧄ 783 dark marigold *(back-stitch: treetop halo)*

⊠ 349 red-orange

⬤ 700 dark kelly green

☑ 414 medium gray

◣ 433 light chocolate brown

310 black *(backstitch: facial features)*

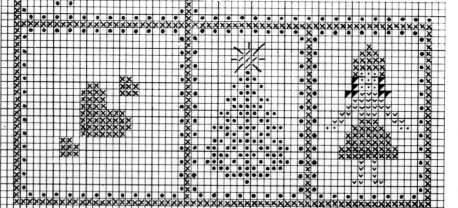

PIXIES
WITH CANDLES

DMC #

◣	973	canary yellow (backstitch: candle glow)
⊠	422	beige
⊡	666	scarlet
⊠	703	light kelly green
	310	black (backstitch: wick and facial features)

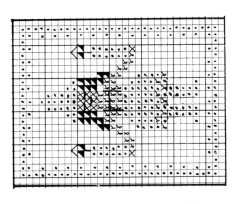

PIXIES ON PARADE

DMC #

⊻	972	light orange
	725	medium marigold (backstitch: treetop glow)
⋰	353	light peach
●	666	scarlet (backstitch: mouths)
◤	798	dark Dresden blue
⊠	906	medium emerald green
▶	435	bright tan

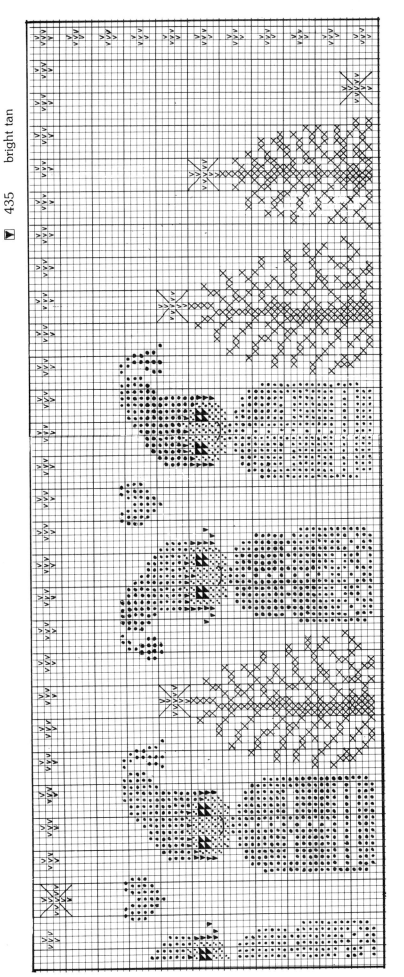

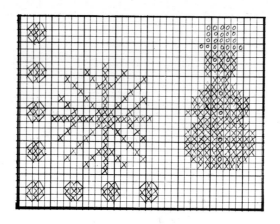

SNOWMEN
AND SNOWFLAKES

Shown in color on the inside front cover.

DMC #

⊠		snow white
⊡	310	black

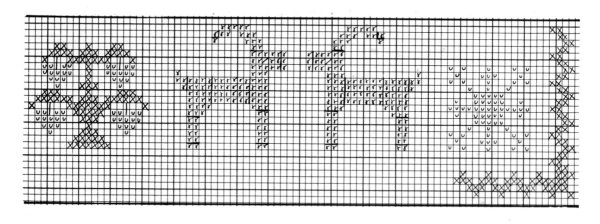

JULBUK
(STRAW REINDEER)

Shown in color on the inside front cover.

DMC #

Ⓤ		snow white
⊠	973	canary yellow
⊠	701	bright kelly green (backstitch: heart hangers)
⊘	310	black
	666	scarlet (backstitch: heavy lines on deer)

LITTLE BOY
WITH A ROBIN

	DMC #					
c		snow white		6	666	scarlet (backstitch: boy's mouth)
·	353	light peach		Z	797	royal blue
0	352	medium peach		8	796	bright royal blue
⁄	973	canary yellow		◢	433	light chocolate brown (backstitch: bird's feet)
Ø	972	light orange				
⫽	608	orange-red (backstitch: bird's beak)				

35

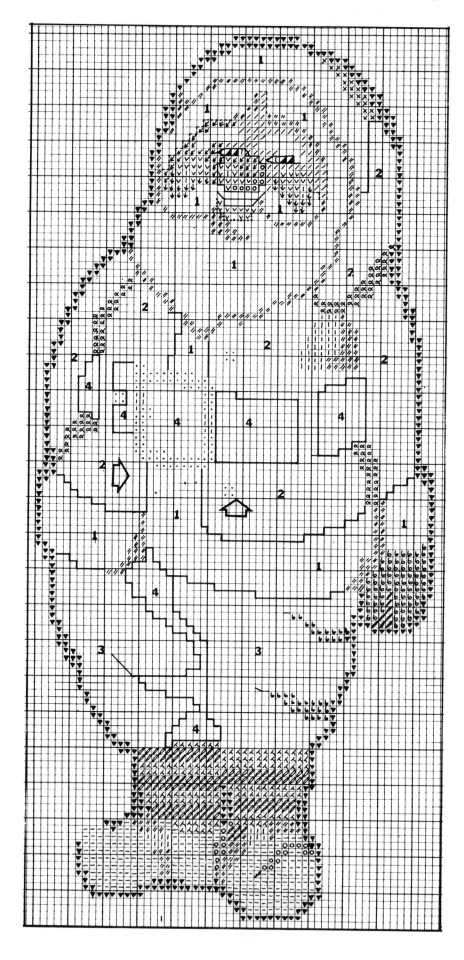

SANTA CLAUS
DMC #

1	⊡		snow white	
	◤	754	medium flesh	
	◿	948	flesh	
	⊟	422	beige	
	⊡	445	light yellow	
	⊻	605	light hot pink	
	⊽	603	dark hot pink (*backstitch: mouth*)	
2	⊠	666	scarlet	
	⍺	304	medium ruby	
	▼	915	dark red-violet	
	⬕	762	pale gray	
	⬕	826	bright blue	
	⬕	702	medium kelly green	
	◪	699	deep kelly green	
	◪	368	light moss green	
3	⊙	842	light brown (*backstitch: on boot*)	
4	◪	839	dark brown (*backstitch: all solid lines*)	
	◪	310	black (*backstitch: around eyes*)	

SANTA CALENDAR

DMC #

⊡		snow white (2)
⊟	945	buff
⋀	972	light orange
⧄	608	orange-red
◩	606	dark orange-red (5)
⊠	741	medium yellow-orange
▼	740	dark yellow-orange
c	352	medium peach
⧄	603	dark hot pink (2) (backstitch: mouth)
ᴣ	718	light red-violet
⊘	553	medium lilac
⧄	552	bright lilac (backstitch: ⊬⊦)
⬀	996	light electric blue
⋎	995	bright electric blue
⧄	415	silver gray (backstitch: edges of beard)
⬰	433	light chocolate brown
⊡	436	medium tan (2)
☑	907	light emerald green
Z	905	bright emerald green (2) (backstitch: ⊬⊦)
6	699	deep kelly green (4)
◉	310	black (2)

When calendar is completed, sew one plastic curtain ring beneath each number and fill each ring with candies, toys or other small trinkets.

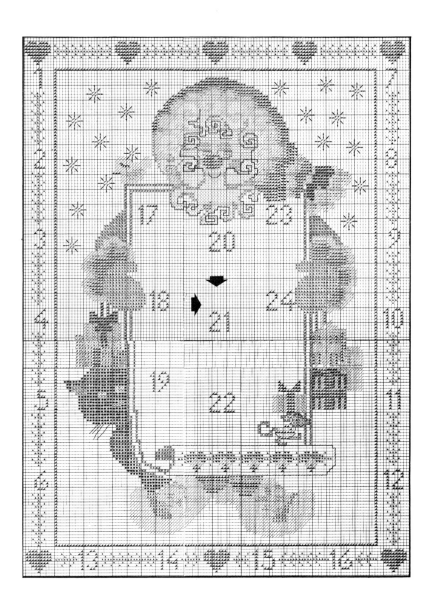

See pages 38-41 for chart.

SANTA CALENDAR
(top left)

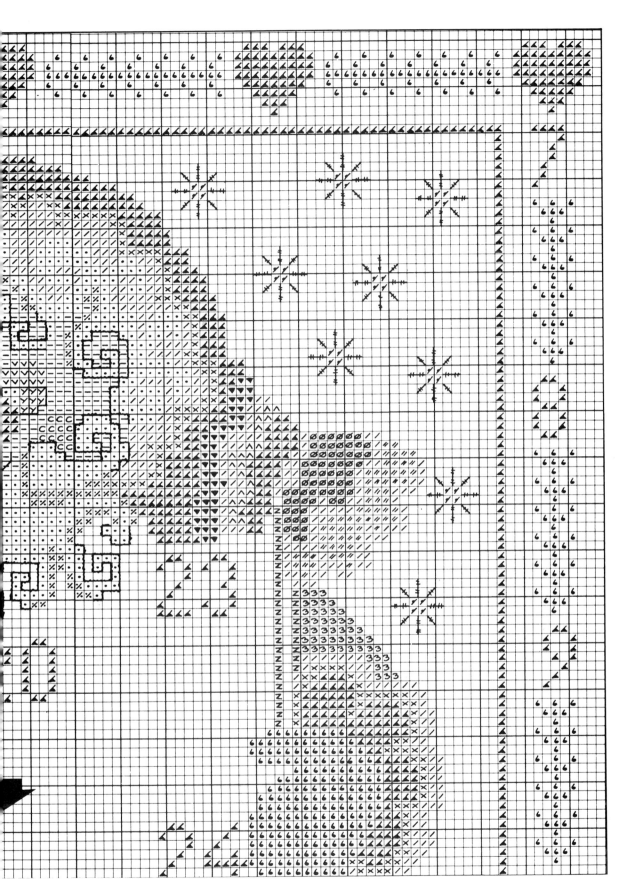

SANTA CALENDAR
(top right)

continued

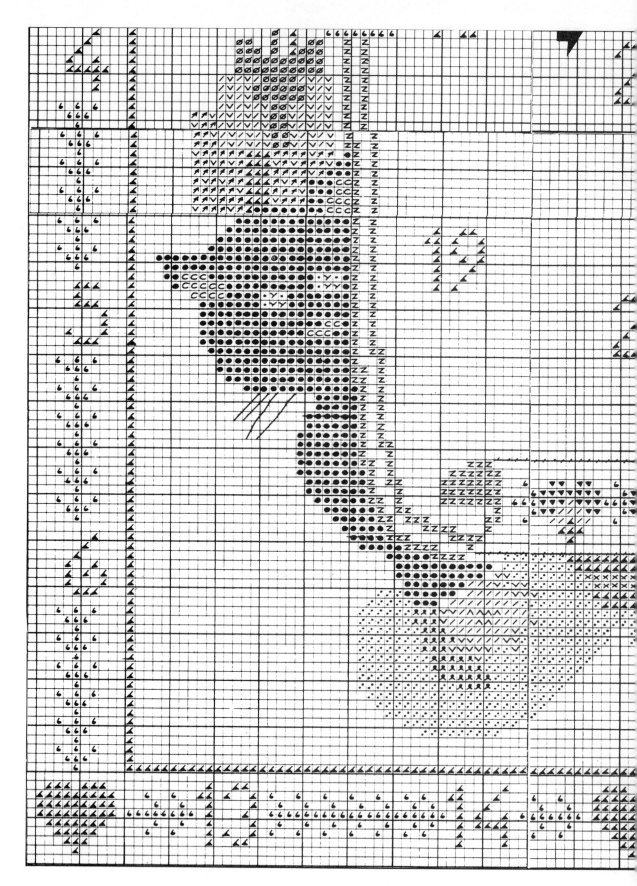

SANTA CALENDAR
(bottom left)

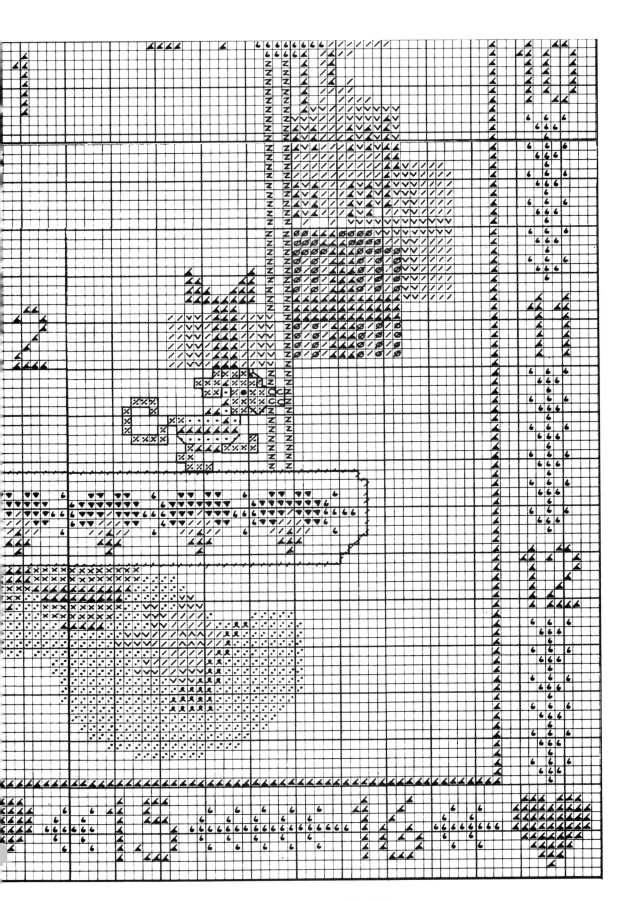

SANTA CALENDAR
(bottom right)

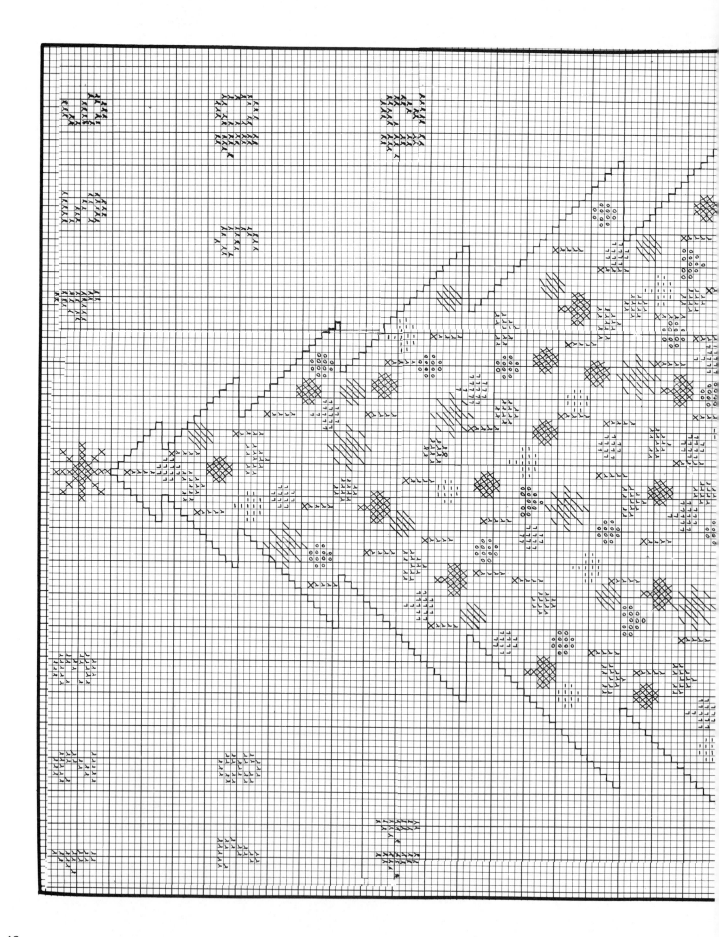

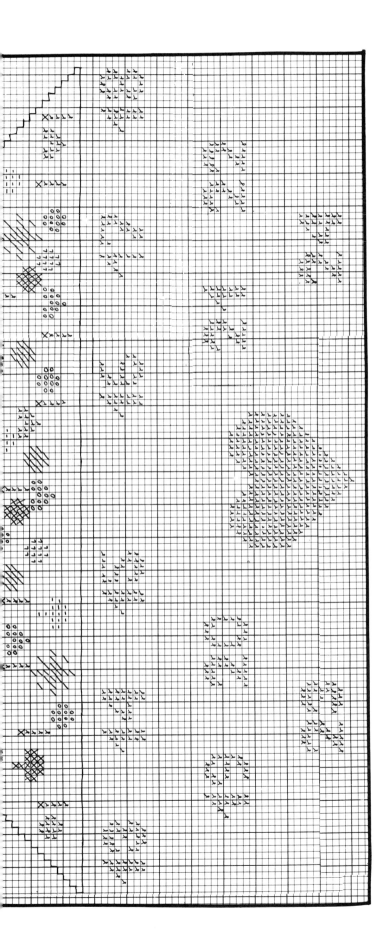

CHRISTMAS TREE CALENDAR

Shown in color on the inside back cover.

When calendar is completed, sew one plastic curtain ring beneath each number and fill each ring with candies, toys or other small trinkets.

	DMC #	
◪		snow white
☒	973	canary yellow (2)
⊙	947	light pumpkin
☒	666	scarlet (4)
⌐	797	royal blue
☐	700	dark kelly green (5)
⌐	210	light lavender

43

POINSETTIA BORDER

DMC #

☑	471	light avocado
·	368	light moss green
☒	989	light grass green
⫿	988	medium grass green *(backstitch: border)*
⍰	987	dark grass green
▼	986	deep grass green
⊙	351	bright peach
Z	350	dark peach
N	349	red-orange
◉	817	cherry red
◪	498	dark ruby
	726	light marigold *(backstitch: around flower centers)*

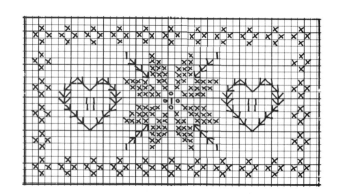

POINSETTIA WITH HEARTS

DMC #

⊡	973	canary yellow
⫿	725	medium marigold
☒	606	dark orange-red
	699	deep kelly green *(backstitch: heavy lines)*

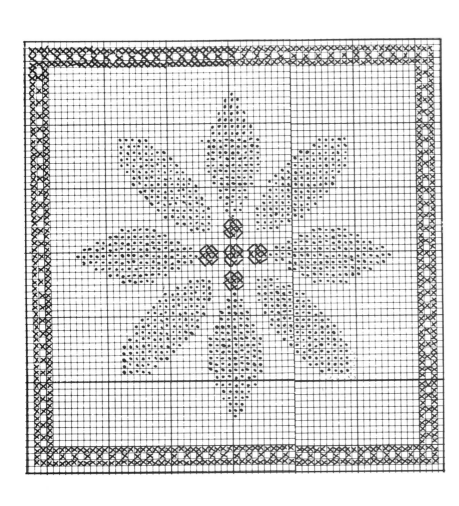

POINSETTIA

Shown in color on the inside back cover.

DMC #
⊡	894	light salmon
⊠	701	bright kelly green
	704	pale kelly green
		(backstitch: around flower centers)

POINSETTIA MOTIF

	DMC #	
⊠	3348	light spring green
⊡	3347	medium spring green
⊟	704	pale kelly green
⊳	702	medium kelly green
⊠	910	deep malachite green
⊠	350	dark peach
⊞	349	red-orange
⊡	817	cherry red

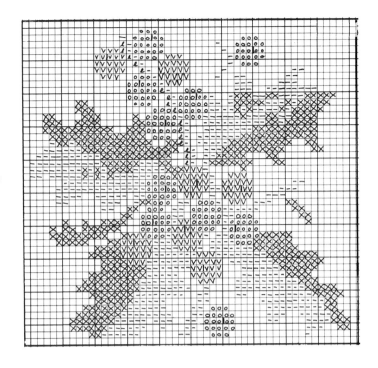

HOLLY

Shown in color on the front cover.

DMC #

⊠	3348	light spring green
☒	3347	medium spring green (*backstitch:* ❙)
⊟	3346	dark spring green
⊙	608	orange-red
☑	606	dark orange-red

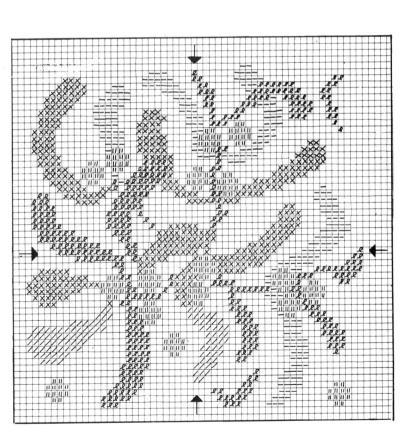

MISTLETOE

DMC #

⊠	3348	light spring green
☒	3347	medium spring green
⊟	3346	dark spring green
☑	3345	hunter green
⊞	504	pale lichen green (*1 strand*) and snow white (*2 strands*)

SIX STRAND EMBROIDERY COTTON (FLOSS) CONVERSION CHART

KEY: T = Possible Substitute   * = Close Match   — = No Match

DMC NO.	ROYAL MOULINÉ	BATES/ANCHOR
White	1001	2
Ecru	8600	926
208	3335*	110*
209	3415*	105
210	3320*	104
211	3410	108*
221	2570	897*
223	2555	894
224	2545	893
225	2540	892
300	8330	352*
301	8315*	349*
304	2415*	47*
307	6005*	289*
309	2525*	42*
310	1002	403
311	4275T	149*
312	3130	147*
315	3130	896*
316	3120	895*
317	1030*	400*
318	1020*	399*
319	5025	246*
320	5015	216*
321	2415	47
322	2530*	978*
326	2530*	59*
327	3365*	101*
333	3355*	119
334	4250T	145
335	2525T	42*
336	4270*	149*
340	—	118
341	—	117
347	2425*	13*
349	2400	13
350	2045*	11
351	2015T	11*
352	2015	10*
353	2010*	8*
355	8095	5968
356	8090	5975*
367	5020	216*
368	5005*	240*
369	5005	213*
370	—	889*
371	—	888*
372	2425*	887*
400	8325*	351
402	8305*	347*
407	8005	882*
413	1025*	401*
414	1020*	400*
415	1015	398
420	8720*	375*
422	8710*	373*
433	8265	371*
434	8215	309
435	8210*	369*
436	8205	363*

DMC NO.	ROYAL MOULINÉ	BATES/ANCHOR
437	8200*	362
444	6155*	291
445	6000	288
451	5365*	399*
452	5365*	399*
453	1015T	397*
469	5255	267*
470	5255*	267
471	5245	266*
472	5240	264*
498	2425T	20*
500	5125	879*
501	5120*	878
502	5110	876
503	5105	875*
504	5100	213*
517	4275T	169*
518	4275T	168*
519	3130	896*
520	3120	895*
522	1030*	400*
523	1020*	399*
524	5025	246*
535	5015	216*
543	2415	47
550	3380*	978*
552	3370*	101
553	3360	98
554	3355*	96*
561	4250T	145*
562	2525T	42*
563	4270*	149*
564	—	203*
580	5935	267*
581	5925	266*
597	4860*	168*
598	4855*	167*
600	2225*	59*
601	2225*	78*
602	2640*	77*
603	2720*	76*
604	2710	75*
605	2155	50*
606	7260	335
608	7255	333*
610	5825T	889*
611	5735T	898
612	8815*	832
613	5605*	956*
632	8530	936*
640	8625	903
642	8620*	392
644	8800	830
645	1115	905*
646	1115*	8581*
647	1110	8581*
648	1100*	900
666	2405	46
676	6250	891
677	—	886*

DMC NO.	ROYAL MOULINÉ	BATES/ANCHOR
680	6260*	901
699	5375	923*
700	5365*	229
701	5365*	227
702	5330	239
703	5320	238
704	5310*	256*
712	8600*	387*
718	3015*	88
720	—	326
721	—	324*
722	—	323*
725	6215	306*
726	6150*	295
727	6135	293
729	6255	890
730	—	924*
731	—	281*
732	5925T	281*
733	—	280*
734	—	279*
738	8245*	942
739	8240*	885*
740	7045	316
741	6125	304
742	6120	303
743	6210	297
744	6110*	301*
745	6105	300*
746	6100	386*
747	4850	210*
754	8075	778*
758	8080	868
760	2035	9*
761	2030	8*
762	1010*	397
772	—	264*
775	4600*	128*
776	2110*	24*
778	3110	968*
780	8215*	310*
781	8215	309*
782	6230	308
783	6220*	307
791	4165*	941*
792	4155	940
793	4155	121
794	4145	120*
796	4340	133*
797	4265*	132*
798	4325	131*
799	4250*	130*
800	4310	128
801	8405	357*
806	4870T	169*
807	4860*	168*
809	4145*	130*
813	4610*	160*
814	2340T	44*
815	2530*	43

DMC NO.	ROYAL MOULINÉ	BATES/ANCHOR
816	2530	44*
817	2415T	19
818	2505*	48
819	2000	892*
820	4345	134
822	8605*	387*
823	4400*	150
824	4225	164*
825	4215	162*
826	4210	161*
827	4605	159*
828	4850	158*
829	5825	906
830	5825*	889*
831	5825T	889*
832	5815	907
833	5815*	874*
834	5810*	874
838	8425*	380
839	8560	380*
840	8555	379*
841	8550	378*
842	8505	376*
844	1115T	401*
869	8720*	944*
890	5025*	879*
891	2135	35*
892	2130	28
893	2125*	27
894	2115T	26
895	5430*	246*
898	8425*	360
899	2515	27*
900	7230*	333
902	—	72*
904	5295*	258*
905	5295	258*
906	5285*	256*
907	5280*	255
909	5370	229*
910	5370*	228*
911	5465*	205*
912	5465	205
913	5460*	209
915	4165*	941*
917	4155T	940
918	4155	121
919	4145	120*
920	4340	133*
921	4265*	132*
922	4325	131*
924	4250*	130*
926	4820*	779*
927	4810T	849*
928	1010T	900*
930	4510	922*
931	4505	921*
932	4500	920*
934	5070T	862*
935	5225T	862*

DMC NO.	ROYAL MOULINÉ	BATES/ANCHOR
936	5260T	269
937	5260	268
938	8430	381
939	4405	127
943	4935*	188*
945	8020*	347*
946	7230*	332*
947	7255*	330*
948	8070	778*
950	8020T	4146
951	8020T	366*
954	5455*	203*
955	5450	206*
956	2170*	40*
957	2160T	40*
958	—	187
959	—	186
961	2515*	76*
962	2515	76*
963	2505	49*
964	5150*	185
966	7040	214*
970	7045	316*
971	—	316
972	6120T	298
973	6015	290
975	8365	355*
976	8355	308*
977	8350	307*
986	5430	246*
987	5020T	244*
988	5295T	243*
989	5405T	242*
991	5165T	189*
992	4925*	187*
993	4915*	186*
995	4710	410
996	4700	433
3011	5525T	845*
3012	5525*	844*
3013	5515	842*
3021	—	382*
3022	—	8581*
3023	—	8581*
3024	1100	900*
3031	—	905*
3032	8620T	903*
3033	8610*	388*
3041	3215*	871
3042	3205*	869
3045	6260T	373*
3046	5810	887*
3047	5805	886*
3051	5530T	846*
3052	5060*	859*
3053	5055*	859*
3064	8005*	914*
3072	4805*	397*
3078	6130	292*
3325	4200	159*

DMC NO.	ROYAL MOULINÉ	BATES/ANCHOR
3326	2115*	25*
3328	2045	11*
3340	—	329
3341	—	328
3345	5025T	268*
3346	5220T	257*
3347	5210*	266*
3348	5270*	265
3350	2220	42*
3354	2210	74*
3362	—	862*
3363	—	861*
3364	8435	843*
3371	—	382
3607	—	87*
3608	—	86
3609	—	85
3685	2335	70*
3687	2325	69*
3688	2320	66*
3689	2310	49
3705	—	35*
3706	—	28*
3708	—	26*
48	9000*	1201*
51	9014	1220
52	9006	1208
53	—	—
57	9002	1203
61	9013T	1218*
62	9000T	1201*
67	—	1211*
69	9002	1218*
75	—	1206*
90	9012T	1217*
91	9008*	1211
92	9011T	1216*
93	9007*	1210*
94	9011*	1216
95	9006T	1208*
99	9005T	1207*
101	9009*	1213*
102	—	1208*
103	—	1210*
104	9012	1217
105	9013*	1218
106	9002T	1203*
107	9003	1204
108	9014*	1220*
111	9007*	1218*
112	9003T	1204*
113	9007*	1210*
114	9010	1215
115	9004	1206
121	9007	1210
122	9010T	1215*
123	9007T	1213*
124	9009	1210*
125	9009	1213
126	9006*	1208*